SAPPHO

Poems and Fragments

Translated by
Stanley Lombardo

Edited by Susan Warden

Introduction by Pamela Gordon

Hackett Publishing Company, Inc.
Indianapolis/Cambridge

Printed in the United States of America

22 21 20 19 3 4 5 6 7

For further information, please address:
Hackett Publishing Company, Inc.
P.O. Box 44937
Indianapolis, IN 46244-0937
www.hackettpublishing.com

Cover design by David Fredrick / Cover photograph by Kirsten Day

Photograph on page 44 reproduced courtesy of Stanley Lombardo and David Fredrick

Library of Congress Cataloging-in-Publication Data
Sappho.
[Selections. English. 2002]
Poems and fragments / translated by Stanley Lombardo ; introduction by Pamela Gordon.
p. cm.
Includes bibliographical references.
ISBN 0-87220-592-4 (cloth)–ISBN 0-87220-591-6 (paper)
1. Sappho–Translations into English. 2. Lesbos Island (Greece)–Poetry. 3. Women–Greece–Poetry. I. Lombardo, Stanley, 1943– II. Title.
PA4408.E5 L6613 2002
884'.01–dc21 2001051548

ISBN-13: 978-0-87220-592- (cloth)
ISBN-13: 978-0-87220-591-8 (paper)

The paper used in this publication meets the minimum requirements of American National Standard for Information Sciences–Permanence of Paper for Printed Library Materials. ANSI Z39.48–1984.

∞

CONTENTS

To my sisters
Nancy and Shirley

smiles playing about your immortal lips

Introduction

Searching for Sappho

Sappho was a Greek poet who lived on the island of Lesbos in the late seventh and early sixth centuries B.C.E. But she is also a construct, a phantom, an icon. Writing about her is a hazardous enterprise. The surviving texts are few (just one full poem, plus the scattered remnants), and the legends are vast. With so few verses and so many myths to go on, a writer inevitably exposes more about her own context than she can reveal about Sappho's.

Even the textual tradition of Sappho's poems has mythic qualities. To start from what might have been the end, legend has it that the early church ordered Sappho's books to be burnt, and thus reduced us to eking out our text of Sappho from scraps and leavings. Whether or not deliberate book-burnings hastened the damage wrought by time and bad luck, the survival of the slender corpus as it exists today is as good a story. More than half of the fragments translated in this volume were lost for over a millennium, to resurface only in the first decades of the 20th century. Some survived in improbable ways. The poem printed here as Sappho's sixth fragment provides a striking example. Broken clay pots were often recycled into "scrap paper" in antiquity, and among the usual receipts and shopping lists one occasionally finds an oddly enchanting message such as: "Leave the saw under the sill of the garden gate" (scratched on a potsherd found in Athens). But one particular broken pot delivers a message of a different order:

down from the mountain top

and out of Crete,
come to me here
in your sacred precinct, to your grove
of apple trees,
and your altars
smoking with incense,

where cold water flows babbling
through the branches,
the whole place
shadowed with roses ...

This text, along with the rest of fragment 6 of this edition, was lost until 1937, when the Italian scholar Medea Norsa published it along with a photograph of the potsherd on which it was written. The text clearly represents the lyrics of a song to Aphrodite, the Greek goddess of erotic love (also called "Cypris," as at the end of this fragment). We know the fragment belongs to Sappho because the text overlaps with three previously known snippets identified explicitly as Sappho's: one quoted in Athenaeus' *The Learned Banquet,* and two others in Hermogenes' *On Kinds of Style* (both Greek writers from the second century C.E.). Like those quotations, the potsherd text was selected and copied at some remove from the poet's own world. The writing on the pottery scrap itself has since deteriorated, but the 1937 photograph reveals a graceful hand, in pen and ink. In many Greek-speaking areas, the usual way to write on a piece of pottery was to scratch the letters with a sharp tool, but pen and ink were the norm in Egypt. Thus the potsherd comes to us not from Lesbos (or Mytilene, as Sappho's island is now called), but presumably from Egypt. The style of handwriting dates the text to somewhere around the second or third century B.C.E.; perhaps 2200–2300 years ago, or three or four hundred years after Sappho.

We cannot know how the lyrics of fragment 6 came to be written on a broken pot. Some scholars imagine a wistful lover wanting to have these words close at hand, as though they might charm an idyllic love scene into reality. Others posit more prosaic contexts: a scribe practicing the trade, or a student obediently responding to dictation. For the other fragments, the circumstances of survival are more transparent. Most of Sappho's extant poems come to us in one of two ways: either as centuries-old scraps of papyrus or parchment (the ancient equivalents to paper); or as quotations in various books that were copied and passed along from era to era. When ancient pieces of papyrus are fortuitously preserved, we usually end up with random snatches of discontinuous text, as in the beginning of fragment 2 in this edition:

climax

lament
with trembling but

The circumstances of the survival of such shreds of text will be discussed later. Quotations, on the other hand, are examples cited by ancient scholars who could not know that their essays and handbooks would outlive the bulk of Sappho's entire corpus. Several of the briefest quotations end with the words "and so on," as though any reader could be expected to know the full text. This type of fragment usually preserves at least a full phrase, as in fragment 4:

> I do not expect my fingers
> to graze the sky

This verse has endured simply because a second-century C.E. scholar was interested in Sappho's unusual spelling of the Greek word for "sky." To cite another example: the rhetorician Hermogenes had quoted "where cold water flows / babbling through the branches" (also in the potsherd fragment quoted above) as an example of a simple description that brings pleasure to the ear, just as beholding the beauty of the actual place would bring pleasure to the eye.

Until the end of the 19th century, such embedded quotations were the only known texts of Sappho. Fortunately, a few of them are just long enough to give us a glimpse of Sappho's genius. One is the only certainly complete poem by Sappho that exists today. This is poem 1 in this edition, which is cited in full by Dionysius of Halicarnassus, a Greek critic and historian who taught rhetoric in Rome in the first century C.E. Praising the way the words are interwoven, Dionysius quotes poem 1 in his essay *On Literary Composition* as an example of "polished and exuberant" expression. The other quotation of significant length is the almost complete fragment 20, which comes to us from *On the Sublime*, a work on literary genius attributed to a shadowy first-century figure called "Longinus." Longinus quotes Sappho 20 as an example of brilliance in isolating and juxtaposing the symptoms of intense erotic desire. Longinus rightly admires how the poem describes the lover's heightened awareness of the convergence (*synodos*) of incongruous emotions. But the poem is also remarkable for the way it captures the triangle: the beloved, the man who has her attention, and the onlooker who possesses only her own overwhelming desire. As Anne Carson writes, the otherwise unidentified man and two women "are three points of transformation on a circuit of possible relationship, electrified by desire so that they touch not touching" (*Eros the Bittersweet*, 16).

The contexts of the shorter embedded fragments are seldom revealing or illuminating, but lines cited for the most mundane of purposes have a way of leaping out at the reader and asserting their presence. Some of the most suggestive short fragments come from Apollonius Dyscolus' work *On Pronouns*, a technical treatise on the forms and uses of pronouns in the various Greek dialects. Apollonius focuses on Sappho's archaic Lesbian-Aeolic spellings of words like "you" and "me," but this interest leads him inadvertently to preserve:

> Towards you, lovely ones, my thoughts
> never change
>
> (fr. 23)

Elsewhere in the same treatise he records:

> You have forgotten me,
> or you love someone else more.
>
> (fr. 58)

Apollonius Dyscolus also gives us the minimalist but pleasing:

> as long as you are willing
>
> (fr. 28)

A discussion of place names by the first-century B.C.E. geographer Strabo yields:

> either Cyprus or Paphos or Panormus
> detains you
>
> (fr. 15)

Here the tone could be one of loss, disappointment, or impatience, but the place names are rich with associations. There was a cult to Aphrodite at Paphos (on the island Cyprus), and Panormus—now Palermo—was a new Phoenician city on Sicily. From the perspective of an archaic Greek islander, Cyprus and Sicily were on opposite ends of the earth.

Also pleasing is the Sapphic quotation included in a scholarly comment (in the margins of a play by Aristophanes) on Lydian dyes:

> sandals
> of fine Lydian make, rainbow-dyed,
> strapped to her feet
>
> (fr. 12)

The many editions and translations of Sappho that appeared during the 19th-century revival of Sappho were based exclusively on such quotations. But in the last years of the 19th century, the corpus of Sappho's poems suddenly began to grow. The potsherd mentioned above is one unexpected latecomer, but most of the new fragments were discovered along with papyrus scraps of Homer, Plato, and other authors in the Roman-era trash heaps of an Egyptian town called Oxyrhynchus. Tattered Greek texts on papyrus (the usual writing material for literature) probably ended up frequently in ancient trash piles elsewhere. But only in the dry climate of Oxyrhynchus were large quantities of legible papyri preserved in this manner, and even in Oxyrhynchus the oldest layers of rubbish are below the water table and thus do not preserve any texts. Some of the Oxyrhynchus papyri contain nearly complete poems, like the justly famous fragment 31, which opens with:

Some say an army on horseback,
some on foot, and some say ships
are the most beautiful things
on this black earth,
                    but I say
it is whatever you love.
                              (fr. 31)

But others are sadly full of holes:

        going to see
Lady Dawn
    arms golden
            (fr. 8)

Many fragments of Sappho continued to emerge from the excavations at Oxyrhynchus between 1897 and 1934, and a few other Sappho texts on papyrus or parchment were also discovered at other sites in Egypt. Although the new texts more than doubled the number of surviving lines of Sappho's poetry, they represent a tiny fraction of the original corpus. Half a millennium after her death, the great library at Alexandria housed a collection of Sappho's poems that consisted of nine papyrus rolls, or books. It is unlikely that Sappho ever conceived of a "complete works" gathered neatly into nine volumes, but the number nine had particular resonances and may thus owe something to Sappho's legendary fame. Later generations of Greeks counted Sappho as the lone woman among the nine Greek lyric poets, and the numbering of the canonical nine mirrored that of the muses, those goddess-daughters of Zeus (traditionally nine in number) who inspire all poetic voices. Another ancient tradition named Sappho herself as the tenth muse.

While British and European archaeologists were discovering new texts by Sappho in Egypt, various women artists were attempting a different sort of Sapphic recovery. Some reinvented Sappho's Lesbos in Paris, but others tried to recuperate a lost Lesbian heritage for women writers by sailing to the island of Lesbos itself. The writers Natalie Barney and Renée Vivien, for example, traveled together to Lesbos via Constantinople in 1904 and set up house there together. Although Barney and Vivien conceptualized Sappho in diverse ways, both regarded her as a model for poetic as well as erotic expression, and they apparently hoped to found an island community of lesbian poets. Vivien spent several seasons in Lesbos, but plans for a modern Sapphic community seem to have faded out even before Vivien's premature death in 1909. A similar impetus was behind Monique Wittig's escape to Mytilene in the 1970s, but her travels seem more metaphorical: ". . . farewell black continent of misery and suffering farewell ancient cities we are embarking for the shining radiant isles and for the green Cytheras, for the dark and gilded Lesbos" (*The Lesbian Body*, New York, 1975, p. 26). Other artists who sailed to Lesbos in the first decades of the century include the American poet H.D. (a.k.a. Hilda Doolittle), whose modernist work was heavily influenced by Sappho's fragments. Isadora Duncan's trips to Greece apparently neglected Lesbos, but included a visit to the cliffs of Leucas on the opposite side of the Greek world, whence, (according to a fictional tradition), Sappho supposedly jumped to her death for unrequited love.

Travel to Sappho's island is considerably easier now than it was a century ago. Mytilene remains beautiful, though today's pilgrims may be as disenchanted by the proliferation of *xenodokia tortes* (fancy resorts, or "cake hotels" as some Greeks call them) as Natalie Barney and Renée Vivien apparently were by the loud music blaring in the harbor of Mytilene when they arrived in 1904. Although traveling to Lesbos gives Sappho's readers an idea of the sea, olive trees, vineyards, and Aegean light that surrounded the poet, we are still over two and a half millennia away when we get there. It is also unlikely—though still possible—that many new fragments of Sappho's poems will emerge from the sands of Egypt. But rather than focusing on the loss and the distance, the reader of Sappho can develop fruitful approaches to the surviving poems.

Reading among the Ruins

First, it is useful to think about different modes of reading a poem and about the various preconceptions and attitudes of the reader. Some of us, picking up a text of Sappho for the first time, might be struck by the immediacy of the emotions expressed in the poems, and we might read as though we were gaining direct access to Sappho despite the distance in centuries and cultures. If we read that way (whether in Greek or in translation), all the books and scholarly articles about Sappho and her culture may seem like an encumbrance that threatens to get between us and the Sapphic voice. An extensive bibliography seldom satisfies a longing to speak with the dead. But many of the traditional scholarly works in fact represent another way of trying to get closer to Sappho. The whole point of much 19th- and early 20th-century classical scholarship on Sappho was to reconstruct the poet's world so as to transport the scholar to Sappho's circle as she sang her songs. Thus the novice reader of Sappho who reads with her heart has something in common with Ulrich von Wilamowitz, the famous 19th-century German classical scholar who devoted so many years to the archaic Greek poets. Wilamowitz had a passionate faith in classics as a science, and he believed that painstaking scholarly work would result in accurate accounts of the lives and minds of the Greek poets.

Perhaps the most rewarding way to read Sappho is by embracing a position somewhere between two extremes: read with one's own desires and interests in the open, but keep one foot in Wilamowitz's study. It is helpful to recognize the hazards of both modes of reading, to remember what those two poles might have in common, and to be open to the possibility of entirely different approaches. One alternative is to read an individual fragment as though we were reading a note in a bottle. Each fragment comes to us against the odds and across the centuries, and none arrives with any original instructions about context or meaning. All we know is that the sender is Sappho (though occasionally we are not even sure of that), and some of us are certain that we are the right recipient. It can help to remember that most of the fragments we have were reattached to the other collected remnants of Sappho's work less than a century ago. It can be useful to know that fragment 6, for example, had no readers for centuries, until its message miraculously arrived in modern Europe.

One reason it is instructive to think of a fragment as an isolated note in a bottle is that we never have a precise archaic context in which to reinsert any particular fragment or poem. Early 20th-century women writers who formed Sapphic writing circles were inspired by an interpretation of the poems to which many scholars of ancient Greek would lend their support: Sappho does indeed seem to have composed her songs within a community of women. And yet our reconstructions of that circle are based primarily on our readings of the fragments themselves. So little is certain, and scholarly consensus often turns out to be built on shifting foundations. There are no biographies of Sappho except the various biographies that other readers have constructed from the fragments and legends. There is no detailed history of archaic Lesbos. If musical scores for the poems ever existed, they are irrevocably lost; all we know for sure is that Sappho played a lyre while she sang. In many ways the generation of Wilamowitz was far too optimistic about how much we can know.

The existing biographies are especially suspect. Generations of readers have assumed that some bare "facts" are unassailable, e.g., that Sappho had a husband named Kerkylas, a brother named Charaxas, and a daughter named Kleis. The notorious problem with the alleged husband is that his name is probably a joke, as Wilamowitz noticed. The ultimate source of the ancient encyclopedia that names Kerkylas specifies that he came from Andros (an actual Greek island). Since Kerkylas sounds a lot like a Greek word for "tail" or "penis" (*kerkos*), and since Andros is also the Greek word for "man," the supposed facts about Sappho's husband were probably the punning inventions of a Greek comic poet. The names for the brother and daughter do not raise similar suspicions, but Kleis probably made her way into the ancient encyclopedia articles directly from the poems. (In their zeal to reconstruct the lives of great artists, ancient biographers often mistook fictional characters for real life people.) In fragment 30 Sappho declares:

> I have a beautiful child, graceful
> as golden flowers, my precious Kleis,
> whom I would not trade for all of Lydia
> or lovely Lesbos

Even if we take this fragment as a factual statement by the historical "Sappho" (not necessarily a good way to read a poem), there is an additional problem with the historicity of Kleis. In recent decades, scholars have noticed that Sappho's word for "child" (*pais*) does not necessarily mean "daughter" or "offspring." Instead, it is a word with a wide range that can refer to any young person, male or female. In addition to being a familiar word for a slave (of any age), it was a common word for a favorite: a boyfriend or a girlfriend. In this poem the adjectives make clear that Kleis is female. But she may be a companion rather than a daughter.

It would be misleading, however, to claim that every surviving text of Sappho is an entirely disembodied voice. Unlike a simple note in a bottle, each text is a fragment of a song that resonates with other surviving songs and poems from the Greek islands and cities. If we read as though a fragment represents Sappho's soul laid bare on the page, we may mistake the words of a character within a song for the expression of Sappho's own desires. Or we may mistake a brilliant work of art for a personal, private outpouring. Here it is useful to recognize that modern assumptions about personal poetry are especially problematic when applied to antiquity. Some classical scholars would go so far as to say that all ancient poetry is public by nature and that there is no such thing as a private voice in archaic Greek texts. Others counter, however, that Sappho—the only significant archaic woman's voice we have—is the great exception. At first reading, we may take her first-person assertions as straightforward confessions from "the real Sappho," but an awareness of other poetry from Sappho's era brings a more informed response to that poetic "I." The seventh-century Archilochus, for example, sounds like an outrageously vengeful individual to readers unaware of the conventions of abuse poetry. Archilochus' personal rage seems to find analogues in the passionate agony of Sappho's compatriot Alkaios and in Sappho's intense desire. But when we read them together we see that some degree of creative fiction is involved. This does not mean that Sappho's tone is artificial or insincere when she writes:

> Truly, I wish I were dead.
> She was weeping when she left me . . .
> (fr. 11)

To the contrary, the first-person declaration pulls us into the poet's orbit and conjures up an intimate scene that is more expansive than a page literally dropped from someone's diary. Sappho even invites us to "believe in" her, for her love poems are not anonymous, but include characters who address a lover named "Sappho" within the poems. Thus fragment 11 continues:

> She was weeping when she left me,
>
> and said many things to me, and said this:
> "How much we have suffered, Sappho.
> Truly, I don't want to leave you."

That we are not simply overhearing an actual conversation becomes even clearer when we consider a poem in which Aphrodite herself addresses Sappho. This is poem 1, in which Sappho calls upon the goddess:

> Shimmering
> iridescent,
> deathless Aphrodite,
> child of Zeus, weaver of wiles,
> I beg you,
> do not crush my spirit with anguish, Lady,
> but come to me now . . .

In this poem, Sappho asserts that she has reason to expect the goddess to appear, for she has descended to Sappho from heaven before, drawn in her chariot "across the bright sky" by sparrows. Aphrodite had smiled on that former occasion and had asked:

> what is it this time?
> why are you calling again?
> (fr. 1)

The wonderful irony here is that Sappho's love goddess is echoing the conventional language of Greek love poetry. As readers of the full range of Greek lyric know, the question "What or who is it *this time*?" (assigned thrice to Aphrodite in this poem) employs a Greek adverb that has a special resonance for lovers. This poignant and not-quite-translatable adverb (*deute*; "again," "this time," "once more") appears with remarkable frequency in Greek love poetry. As a recent article by Sarah Mace points out, we have this adverb in a very particular formula in several poems by four different archaic poets. Seven of those poems begin with the same three words: *Eros deute me* (Eros, once more . . . me). Eros, whence we get our word *erotic*, is Desire personified, and a distant relative of his Roman semiequivalent, Cupid. He is a companion to Aphrodite, and is often described as her divine son, equipped with weapons and wings. In the poems in the "Eros, once more . . ." series, and in Greek poetry in general, Eros is a serious force to be reckoned with. Recognizing something so simple as a repeated three-word formula gives us a glimpse of an ancient context: something like an ongoing poetry slam in which the archaic poets competed to describe Eros adequately and to produce the best image to depict his attack. Thus a sixth-century poet named Anacreon attempted to trounce his predecessors by delivering: "With a huge hammer Eros this time has struck me like a blacksmith and plunged me in an icy torrent" (Denys Page, *Poetae Melici Graeci,* p. 413). In Sappho's own direct engagement with this tradition, Eros is both more subtly distressing and more welcome:

> Eros once more limbslackener makes me shudder
> sweetbitter irresistible creeping
> (fr. 71)

Other poets applied the adjective "limbslackener" (*lusimeles*) to Eros, Sleep, Death, sickness, and wine; but "sweetbitter" (*glukupikron*) is apparently Sappho's own coinage. As Anne Carson suggests, here the word *deute* (translated in this fragment as "once more") marks both the startled widening of the eyes and the immediate narrowing as one thinks, "Oh, *this* again." To quote Carson, the word *deute* appears "like one long, rather wild sigh at the beginning of the poem, as the lover perceives her attacker and understands that it is (oh no!) already too late (not again!) to avoid desire" (*Eros the Bittersweet*, p. 119).

To return to Sappho poem 1: By attributing the love poets' shared language to the love goddess herself, Sappho brings a new twist to the tradition. An awareness of that twist helps bring into focus Sappho's treatments of Eros and Aphrodite. By echoing Sappho's own diction, Aphrodite is simultaneously siding with the poet and taunting her with her own words. Or does Sappho have such a tight connection to Aphrodite that the goddess competes with her to pin down the laws of desire? Elsewhere, we find the lone line: "I talked with you in a dream, Aphrodite" (fr. 32). Looking to other fragments, one hears both the confidence in Sappho's voice as she sings: "come to me here" (fr. 6), and the risk involved: "do not crush my spirit with anguish" (poem 1). The danger of having Aphrodite against one is also apparent in the fragment that pleads: "O Cypris, / may she find you more bitter still" (fr. 7). Although the text is uncertain, a glimmer of Aphrodite's sinister power may also shine through the damaged papyrus in fragment 57: "but you, Cypris, / disposing of the evil woman".

An indication of the varied meanings and powers of Aphrodite is evident too in the array of names with which Sappho addresses her: "Aphrodite," "child of Zeus," "weaver of wiles," "Lady," "Cypris," "Cytherea" (the latter two names referring to two islands with rival claims of being Aphrodite's birthplace). Aphrodite's companion Eros also comes in many guises. We have already seen that he is "sweetbitter," "irresistible," and "creeping." A second-century C.E. scholar named Pollux tells us that in another lost poem Eros arrives from heaven wearing a purple mantle.

Also in the second century, a public lecturer named Maximus of Tyre quotes this Sapphic fragment:

> Eros has shaken my mind,
> wind sweeping down the mountain on oaks
> (fr. 26)

At the same point in that lecture (*Orations* 18.9), Maximus of Tyre gives us a glimpse of another side of Sappho's Eros by mentioning that Socrates calls Eros a "sophist," and Sappho calls him a *mythoplokos*, "a story-weaver." The combined reference to Socrates and Sappho gives us a notion of Sappho's reputation for wisdom, but significant too is the fact that both authorities are calling Eros "a talker." Socrates' label for Eros implies that Desire traffics in verbal ploys and persuasion (or even false advertising), but Sappho's name for Eros stresses the attractiveness of his stories. By calling Desire *mythoplokos*, Sappho reminds us how love needs a narrative and the lover needs an imagination. Sappho's name for Eros, "the story-weaver," also points to one of the most essential qualities of Sappho's own lyrics. The sounds and shapes of her verses are inimitable, but often it is the sheer strength of narrative that comes through on the most fragile of fragments. Fragment 24, which describes in intricate detail the marriage of Hector and Andromache, is the only fragment that gives us an idea of Sappho's sustained handling of a complex narrative. But even in the shortest fragments, Sappho supplies us with the verbal images that have fed the imaginations of Sappho's readers: Anactoria's way of walking, the treachery of Atthis, the woman who rivals Helen, the man "like a god" impassively listening to a voice that is nearly killing the other listener.

In some eras of Sappho's varied afterlife, readers and scholars and novelists have wanted to shape Sappho's fragments into a single connected narrative. Often the result has been a different and less compelling sort of storytelling, with Sappho losing one lover after another and finally leaping to her death from the cliffs of Leucas. Or there is the scholarly feat of bringing everything together into one unified narrative in which Sappho is a teacher who sends successive generations of lovely girls off to marriage. There is already a spark of this tradition in the works of the Roman poet Ovid, but its modern reincarnation began with Wilamowitz and an earlier scholar named Welcker. Notoriously, Wilamowitz brought even fragment 20 into this scheme: the sweetly talking girl as the bride, the godlike man as the groom, and Sappho as the stricken wedding singer.

Better to abandon the tangled mass of biography and return to the idea of the isolated message. We might miss the poem if we focus on constructing a life of Sappho in which she figures as a victim of unrequited love. Instead of trying to weave the fragments too closely together, why not take each one as it comes, remembering that a poem can resonate with other poems without becoming an entry in a single narrative? We might understand loss and absence, not as the tragic patterns of Sappho's own life, but as qualities inherent to her depiction of Eros. We might consider that love is like Sappho's apple:

> Like the sweet apple reddening on the topmost branch,
> the topmost apple on the tip of the branch,
> and the pickers forgot it,
> well, no, they didn't forget, they just couldn't reach it.
> (fr. 69)

Upper Case, Lower Case: Was Lesbian Sappho a lesbian?

Ancient sources refer to an entire papyrus roll of Sappho's wedding songs, or *Epithalamia.* The fragment that celebrates a splendidly tall bridegroom with the famous verse "Raise high the roofbeam, carpenters" (fr. 42) clearly belongs to that genre. So too, the poem in which a bride addresses her virginity:

> Virginity, virginity, where are you going,
> deserting me?

and her virginity replies:

> I shall come to you no more, come no more.
> (fr. 45)

These are fragments from songs Sappho sang to celebrate unions between men and women. To many readers it will be obvious that some of Sappho's fragments also celebrate the erotic desire of one woman for another. Newcomers to classical scholarship, however, may be surprised to learn how problematic the shift from Lesbian to lesbian can be. Nineteenth- and early 20th-century studies that made Sappho out to be a heterosexual matron who ran an island school for girls have receded into the past, but the issues remain complex.

In his 1955 commentary on the archaic poets of Lesbos, the British classical scholar Denys Page discusses Sappho's desire in tones that seem remarkably forthright for the 1950s:

> If we read Sappho without prejudice, we observe that she is deeply moved by the physical graces of young women. It is a lover's passion, not sisterly affection or maternal benevolence, which Sappho describes in fragment 31 [fragment 20 this edition], the overwhelming emotion of intensest love. (p. 143)

In the same chapter, however, Page attempts (with evident indignation) to deny the "accusation" that Sappho "was addicted to the perversion which the modern world names after her native island" (ibid.). It soon becomes clear that Page's acceptance of homoerotic "inclination" does not extend to homoerotic "practice" (p. 144). His Sappho experiences desire as "wind sweeping down the mountain on oaks," but she has no partner when she arranges her "limbs on soft cushions." Page acknowledges that a few references in ancient comedies and biographies suggest that there were women on Sappho's island who were especially interested in erotic encounters with other women. But he finds "not a word which connects herself or her companions with them, and at most half a word which reveals her awareness of their existence." That half-word seems to shake Page's confidence. What is the word? In a footnote he explains that five mangled letters might represent "a word of quite unusual coarseness, referring to practices about which silence is almost universally maintained." Professor Page looks for alternative readings for each of the five letters and considers the possibility that Sappho's compatriot Alkaios, and not our Sappho, is the author; he finally admits that the evidence for Sappho's lack of innocence seems unavoidable. Page offers no translation, but a Greek dictionary reveals that the offending letters (*olisb-*) in Oxyrhynchus Papyrus 2291 are possibly the beginning of a word for a sex toy. Perhaps it is not too surprising that a contemporary of Sigmund Freud would assume that a word for "dildo" should reveal Sappho's knowledge of lesbian sex. The fragment is omitted from Lombardo's translation, not out of fear of offending our gentle readers, but simply because it is so fragmentary as to be illegible. In fact, the verse might not refer to anything sexual at all; another interpretation is that the fragment describes lyre strings that are happy to receive the plectrum. But to return to Page and his own sense of decorum: Page knows that "penis substitutes" were mentioned for laughs in

Greek comedies, but would he read Lysistrata's regret that she lacks even an *olisbos* (while her husband is away at war) as "lesbian" evidence? (See Aristophanes' *Lysistrata*, line 109.)

Page's commentary records a curious mixture of circumlocution and frankness, of homophobia and openness. But half a century later, it is still difficult to describe Sapphic "sexuality" (to use another word with a vexed history) without writing something that future readers will find peculiar, misguided, or simply incorrect. Prudishness, chivalry, misogyny, and homophobia—not to mention the fragmentary nature of the texts, or the lack of historical information—are not the only obstacles. Much of the difficulty stems from the fact that desire itself has no stable, cross-cultural value. Erotic desire may seem universal and timeless, but its meaning varies wildly from culture to culture, from language to language, from person to person. Few things are more culturally contingent than love and sex.

An obvious problem with naming Sappho a "lesbian" is that the ancient Greeks seem generally not to have thought about desire in terms of sexual orientation. A seventh-century Greek might assume that erotic desire takes many forms, but it is unlikely a Greek thought in terms of fixed categories that can be neatly translated into modern terms such as "lesbian," "bisexual," or "heterosexual." Thus it is not surprising that some of Sappho's lyrics are ambiguous about the gender of the object of desire; it is also not surprising that the ambiguity sometimes lurks quietly behind the verses. Fragment 36, for example, seems clear-cut in English:

> Sweet mother, I can no longer work the loom.
> Slender Aphrodite has made me fall in love with a boy.

The word translated here as "boy" (*pais*) is likely to mean just that: a young male object of desire. But although *pais* is a very common word for "boy," it appears here with no gender-specific article or adjective. Thus it is just possible that Sappho's original poem was not so specific: our distracting boy might be a girl. Elsewhere we find similarly remarkable abstraction. Particular objects of desire—and the response to the beloved's distinct and individual qualities—emerge from Sappho's fragments with clarity and precision. When Sappho generalizes, however, the gender of the beloved disappears: "but I say / it is whatever you love" (fr. 31).

When we move beyond the modern preoccupation with sexual preference or orientation, the issues become more complicated. Readers in search of evidence for a female sexuality that differs radically from men's sexuality in antiquity have often turned to Sappho. And many scholars believe that Sappho's fragments do indeed view desire from a distinctly female angle. Some have claimed that Sappho presents an erotics of reciprocity and mutuality that stands in stark contrast to other archaic poets' themes of masculine pursuit and feminine submission. Many have asserted that Sappho's poetry describes a community far removed from the male-centered, competitive world of archaic Greece. For many contemporary readers, such interpretations of Sapphic desire are essential to an understanding of Sappho as a poet of lesbian desire.

Poem 1, for instance, has often been described as an example of mutual passion. There Aphrodite responds to the lover's plea for help by assuring her that the beloved will soon become a lover:

> "Whom now
> should I persuade to love you?
> Who is wronging you, Sappho?
> She may run now, but she'll be chasing soon.
> She may spurn gifts, but soon she'll be giving."

Where some readers see reciprocity, however, others see a desire for domination and vengeance. The latter interpretation stresses the import of Aphrodite's next words:

> "She may not love now, but soon she will,
> willing or not."

In this reading, the last line of the poem ("fight at my side, Goddess") further links Sappho with the male lyric poets, who commonly describe love as military conquest. We can even go one step further, and read the prayer to Aphrodite as a plea for justice (as does Anne Carson in her essay, "The Justice of Aphrodite in Sappho 1"). In this reading, Aphrodite is not promising reconciliation with the fleeing beloved. Rather, she is assuring the plaintiff that this unresponsive object of desire will soon suffer a similar plight. She too will fall in love, and she will find out how it feels to be spurned.

Readers who agree that some of the fragments describe an agonistic view of love need not abandon the search for a poetics of lesbian desire. A position articulated by the early 20th-century poet H.D. provides a case in point. H.D. celebrated Sappho's departures from heterosexual norms as H.D. knew them, but in her reading of the fragments, she did not find mutuality, equality, and reciprocity. Instead, H.D. valued Sappho's arrogance. In an essay she wrote between 1918 and 1920, H.D.

characterized Sappho as: "Indifferent—full of caprice—full of imperfection—intolerant." ("The Wise Sappho," p. 59). H.D. was especially taken with fragment 38:

> What farm girl has seduced you?
> Draped in burlap,
> she doesn't even know to pull her rags
> down over her ankles.

Athenaeus, the second-century C.E. writer who quotes these lines, tells us that they were addressed to a woman named Andromeda, who figures elsewhere as some sort of rival to Sappho:

> Atthis,
> you have come to hate the very thought of me,
> and you run off to Andromeda.
>
> (fr. 59)

Reveling in her discovery that a woman can be blunt and sardonic, H.D. imagines Sappho's eyes twisting as she writes, "the spark of mockery beneath the half-closed lids" ("The Wise Sappho," p. 59). More recently, Page duBois has also suggested that the contempt expressed for a ragged farm girl in fragment 38 should help us to grasp Sappho's interest in power and to recognize that her voice is dominant and aristocratic.

Another way to approach the issue of homoeroticism is to ask if Sappho's lyrics are queer. Here a sense of history is also helpful. By the time of the early Roman empire (first century C.E.), it seems clear that some readers understood Sappho not simply as a love poet, but as a lover of women, and that they saw Sapphic desire for women as something peculiar. Some Roman texts even express disgust and contempt for a type of monstrous woman the Romans called a *tribas* (plural: *tribades*). *Tribades* haunt graveyards and run wild at night, and the height of their monstrousness is that they have sex with other women. This is the general context in which Ovid composed a fictional letter from Sappho to a young male lover named Phaon (*Heroides* 15). In that epistolary poem, Sappho renounces the lovers she had on Lesbos as though her love for women had been something wrong:

> Lesbian islanders,
>   Married, engaged,
> Lesbians catalogued on my Aeolian lyre,
> Lesbians loved to my disgrace,
> crowd around to hear my zither no more.

In this poem, Ovid plays on the place name: The word "Lesbian" is still simply a geographical term, and yet Ovid knows that his readers have opinions about the supposedly scandalous sexual practices of Lesbian women.

Sappho's lyrics know nothing of this sort of censure. Although we cannot reconstruct the context in detail, the tone of Sappho's fragments suggests that her community understood eros between women as something entirely affirmative. Her lyrics assert an intense interest in desire and pleasure, and they assert an awareness of differing from others by placing such a high value on love: "but I say / it is whatever you love" (fr. 31). But Sappho's lyrics do not mark desire between women as something odd or subversive. As the readings of H.D. and of Page duBois make clear, Sappho occupies a position of authority. When she calls upon Aphrodite, she sings with the conviction that she has her audience and heaven itself on her side.

In this sense it seems that Sappho does not become queer until archaic Lesbos becomes history. But if there is any hint of subversion or queerness in Sappho's poems, the peculiarity may reside in her handling of male attractiveness. In fragment 44, Sappho sings:

> To what shall I compare you, dear bridegroom?
> I shall compare you to a slender sapling.

In Homer's *Odyssey,* Odysseus had compared the princess Nausikaa to a graceful young tree. Sappho, however, turns a stock description of a pretty girl into praise of a man. Elsewhere, Sappho seems to resist the emphasis on physical beauty that is so pervasive in Greek culture:

> He who is beautiful is so only when seen,
> But he who is good will be beautiful at once.
> (fr. 51)

And yet in some fragments, Sappho aligns herself with conventional views, as in the fragment that ends:

> For I will not endure an affair
> In which I am older than the man.
> (fr. 62)

The name of Sappho has meant a great deal to generations of poets, novelists, scholars, lovers, and dreamers, but it has never been a stable signifier. If one wants to take Sappho as a model for desire among women, it is best to read with an acute awareness of the distance and difference between her world and one's own. Ironically, some of the most appealing attempts to describe Sapphic desire in modern terms are those that indulge in deliberate anachronism. In Marguerite Yourcenar's *Fires* (written in French in 1935), the character named Sappho is a 20th-century circus acrobat. One of her beloveds is Attys, a girl with a fake otter coat, holes in her shoes, and soot stains and tears on her face (see Atthis in fragments 49 and 59, above). Attys accepts refuge with Sappho and takes a childish delight in the fixtures in Sappho's hotel bathroom. When Attys slips away with a man who smells of tobacco and cologne, Sappho searches for years—at circuses, Middle Eastern hotels, the Salvation Army. Though Attys herself is forever missing, every one of her traits remains vivid and certain. And before Attys, there was Anactoria:

> Anactoria's love brought her the taste of French fries eaten by handfuls in amusement parks, of rides on the wooden horses of carousels, and brought her the sweet feel of straw, tickling the neck of the beautiful girl lying down in haystacks. (pp. 118–19)

In this meditation on eros and absence, Yourcenar has no interest in historical verisimilitude. She focuses instead on the significance of detail and the power of memory in Sappho's fragments.

Suggestions for Further Reading

A vast library is available for scholars and students working on Sappho today. This list includes only a few widely available works in English (organized into rough and overlapping rubrics), most of which include extensive bibliographies. Three very different introductions to Sappho are: Page duBois, *Sappho Is Burning* (University of Chicago Press, 1995); Jane Snyder, *The Woman and the Lyre* (Southern Illinois University Press, 1989); and Margaret Williamson, *Sappho's Immortal Daughters* (Harvard University Press, 1995). All three are accessible to the Greekless reader, but the latter two survey recent scholarship with the general reader especially in mind. Readers interested in the construction of love and erotic desire in Sappho should also consult: Anne Pippin Burnett, *Three Archaic Poets* (Harvard University Press, 1983); Anne Carson, *Eros the Bittersweet* (Princeton University Press, 1986), and Claude Calame, *The Poetics of Eros in Ancient Greece* (translated by Janet Lloyd, Princeton

University Press, 1999). All three of these books discuss Sappho with reference to other archaic lyric poets. Carson's is an especially original and witty meditation accessible to the general reader; Burnett and Calame are intended more for advanced students and scholars. Denys Page's *Sappho and Alcaeus* (Oxford University Press, 1955, 1979) is still useful and informative. For various approaches to the question of whether Sappho's poetic voice is specifically female, lesbian, or woman-identified, see duBois; Snyder, *Lesbian Desire in the Lyrics of Sappho* (Columbia University Press, 1997); Williamson; John Winkler, *The Constraints of Desire* (Routledge, 1990); the many essays collected in Ellen Greene's two edited volumes, *Reading Sappho* and *Re-Reading Sappho* (University of California Press, 1996). On readings of Sappho in bygone eras (including discussions of sexuality), see Joan DeJean, *Fictions of Sappho* (University of Chicago Press, 1989), Yopie Prins, *Victorian Sappho* (Princeton University Press, 1999), and Greene's *Re-Reading Sappho*. Those interested in the notion that desire and gender are performed and constructed (rather than universal or innate) should consult Page duBois's introduction to *Sappho Is Burning* and the theoretical work of Judith Butler, Michel Foucault, Eve Sedgwick and their many readers and critics. Although they do not treat Sappho extensively, Kenneth Dover's *Greek Homosexuality* (Harvard University Press, 1978) and David Halperin's *One Hundred Years of Homosexuality* (Routledge, 1989) are also relevant. The most recent materials on Sappho can be found conveniently by searching the bibliographies available on the Diotima website: <http://www.stoa.org/diotima/>.

Pamela Gordon
University of Kansas

Additional Bibliography

Carson, Anne. "The Justice of Aphrodite in Sappho 1." Transactions of the American Philological Association 110 (1980): 135–42.

Greene, Ellen. *Reading Sappho*. Berkeley: University of California Press, 1996.

Hallett, Judith. "Sappho and Her Social Context: Sense and Sensuality." *Signs* 4 (1979): 447–64.

H.D., *Notes on Thought and Vision & The Wise Sappho* San Francisco: City Lights Books, 1982.

Mace, Sarah. "Amour Encore! The Development of *deute* in Archaic Greek Lyric." *Greek, Roman, and Byzantine Studies* 34 (1993): 335–64.

Page, Denys, ed. *Poetae Melici Graeci.* Oxford: Oxford University Press, 1962.

Prins, Yopie. *Victorian Sappho.* Princeton: Princeton Unversity Press, 1999.

Skinner, Marilyn B. "Woman and Language in Archaic Greece, or, Why Is Sappho a Woman?" In *Feminist Theory and the Classics,* edited by N. S. Rabinowitz and A. Richlin, 125–44. New York: Routledge, 1993.

Welcker, F. G. *Sappho von einem herrschenden Vorurteil befreyt.* In *Kleine Schriften zur Griechischen Litteraturgeschichte,* 2:80–144. Bonn: Eduard Faber, 1845. [First published as a book in Gottingen, 1816].

Wilamowitz-Moellendorf, Ulrich von. *Sappho und Simonides: Untersuchungen uber griechische Lyriker.* Berlin: Weidmann, 1913.

Wittig, Monique. *The Lesbian Body.* Translated from the French by David Le Vay. Boston: Beacon Press, 1986.

Yourcenar, Marguerite. *Fires.* Translated from the French by Dorie Katz in collaboration with the author. New York: Farrar Straus Giroux, 1981.

Translator's Note

Mary Barnard put it well for the Sappho translator: "The texts vary to such an extent and have been emended by so many hands that the translator has a choice of words and meanings for almost every line" (*Sappho: A New Translation*, Berkeley: University of California Press, 1958, p. 105). I've decided just to follow the most recent critical edition, David Campbell's fairly conservative text in the Loeb series (*Greek Lyric, Volume 1: Sappho and Alcaeus*, Cambridge: Harvard University Press, 1982). Unlike some previous editors, Campbell does not indulge in much speculative reconstruction. Where my translation differs from Campbell's main text, which is not often, I am either using one of the variant readings he prints in his *apparatus criticus* or simply allowing myself to diverge from a literal rendering.

When I began this project I found myself coming to Campbell's Greek text of Sappho as a pure, received text, that is, as if I had come across it published, perhaps in a contemporary poetry journal, without any introduction or biographical note, as a set of two hundred or so brief, numbered pieces. This entailed, among other things, largely dropping out of consideration any biographical information we may or may not possess and, further, regarding the fragments as esthetic wholes, complete in their fragmentariness and not in need of conjectural restoration. I like Page duBois's notion of Sappho's poetry as a Lacanian "body in pieces" and her shift of focus from reconstitution of classical lost wholes to our momentary and receding relationship to the shattered fragments of the past (*Sappho Is Burning*, Chicago: University of Chicago Press, 1995). In the end, though, I have engaged in some kind of reconstitution, as a translator must, and have constructed something—a poetry book—out of the seventy-three pieces I have chosen to translate, all that I could make poetic sense of. These number about a third of those in Campbell's text, but since they include all of the longer pieces, they account for by far the major part of Sappho's surviving poetry. Having translated these pieces, I felt compelled to order and arrange them into a collection with some kind of esthetic coherence. Every poet or artist who has arranged pieces for publication or for an exhibition can understand the enjoyment this process brings and how important it is for an appreciation of the total body of work.

My poetics as a translator of these poems have been somewhat fluid. My interest in the rhythmic phrase as the main structural element should be apparent; that interest has been reinforced by the gaps in the text that often leave us with only these beautiful, isolated limbs. I sometimes deliberately treat a more or less intact passage as if composed of fragments that reduce to rhythmic phrases. I have made no attempt to follow, although I do sometimes suggest, Sappho's various lyric meters. (Richmond Lattimore did a fine job of translating Sappho in approximations of her meters in his *Greek Lyrics*, Chicago: University of Chicago Press, 1955). The comment of Dionysius of Halicarnassus on the first poem in this collection, "Words are juxtaposed and interwoven according to certain natural affinities and groupings of letters," is something I understand in Sappho and take as a basic principle of composition—the subtle texturing of sound that goes beyond what is usually understood by euphony. See the first three words of my translation of Sappho 1 for an obvious example. And I am ever mindful of performative qualities, quality of voice, changes of voice—how I would read or have read a passage to an audience and scripting that reading on the printed page.

I first read Sappho in Greek in 1964 with Emmett Bienvenu, S.J., as an undergraduate at Loyola University in New Orleans. I owe a debt of gratitude to him, first, and then to my own students and colleagues at the University of Kansas and elsewhere with whom I have read Sappho and talked about her poetry over the years. This translation has benefited enormously from a number of people who have offered specific suggestions. I would like to acknowledge and thank especially Susan Warden, whose editorial help and esthetic sense have been invaluable. I want to thank also Pamela Gordon, both for her splendid Introduction and for her general support. Thanks also to Linda Mann for her help in compiling the notes on ancient sources and to Doug Hutchinson for compiling the concordance that appears on p. xxviii. And special gratitude goes to David Fredrick for designing the cover and editing the picture of my sister, Nancy Brehm, which appears opposite fragment 49. This book honors my wife, Judy Roitman, and is dedicated to my sisters, Nancy Brehm and Shirley Treichel, all of whose voices are ever in my ears, and who have taught me much about love.

Stanley Lombardo
University of Kansas

Campbell-Lombardo Concordance

Campbell	Lombardo	Campbell	Lombardo
1	1	57	38
2	6	58	66
3	56	62	18
4	17	63	19
5	57	65	21
6	8	81	35
7	9	92	25
8	10	94	11
9	53	96	54
15	7	98	17
16	31	101	52
17	3	102	36
21	2	104	48
22	60	105	69
23	33	107	40
27	37	110	43
30	34	111	42
31	20	114	45
34	22	115	44
35	15	121	62
36	16	122	46
37	64	126	63
38	65	129	58
39	12	130	71
40	13	131	59
41	23	132	30
44	24	134	32
45	28	135	68
46	27	136	67
47	26	137	50
48	61	140	14
49	49	146	39
50	51	151	72
51	41	154	70
52	4	168b	73
55	5	168c	29
56	55		

Poems and Fragments

1

Shimmering,
iridescent,
deathless Aphrodite,
child of Zeus, weaver of wiles,
I beg you,
do not crush my spirit with anguish, Lady,
but come to me now, if ever before
you heard my voice in the distance
and leaving your father's golden house
drove your chariot pulled by sparrows
swift and beautiful
over the black earth, their wings a blur
as they streaked down from heaven
across the bright sky—

and then you were with me, a smile
playing about your immortal lips
as you asked,
what is it this time?
why are you calling again?
And asked what my heart in its lovesick raving
most wanted to happen:
"Whom now
should I persuade to love you?
Who is wronging you, Sappho?
She may run now, but she'll be chasing soon.
She may spurn gifts, but soon she'll be giving.
She may not love now, but soon she will,
willing or not."

Come to me again now, release me
from my agony, fulfill all
that my heart desires, and fight for me,

fight at my side, Goddess.

2

climax

lament
with trembling but
already the old man's skin
eating all around
takes wing pursuing
illustrious lady
taking
sing to us

the violet-breasted

she wanders

3

May your graceful form glimmer
close to me as I pray, Lady Hera,
goddess beseeched by Atreus' sons,
glorious kings

who accomplished many heroic deeds
first at Troy and then on the sea
but could not complete their journey's end
here to this island

until they called upon you and Zeus
and Thyone's lovely son Dionysus.
So also now be gracious to me
as to them of old.

Holy and fair
maidens
around

to be

to reach

4

I do not expect my fingers
to graze the sky

5

When you are dead you will lie forever unremembered
and no one will miss you, for you have not touched the roses
of the Pierian Muses. Invisible even in the house of Hades,
you will wander among the dim dead, a flitting thing.

6

down from the mountain top

and out of Crete,
come to me here
in your sacred precinct, to your grove
of apple trees,
and your altars
smoking with incense,

where cold water flows babbling
through the branches,
the whole place
shadowed with roses,
sleep adrift down
from silvery leaves
an enchantment

horses grazing in a meadow
abloom with spring flowers
and where the breezes blow sweetly,

here, Cypris,
delicately in golden cups
pour nectar
mixed for our festivities.

7

blessed one
lovely braids

O Cypris,
may she find you more bitter still
and Dorikha not boast her desire
come to fulfillment a second time.

8

going to see
Lady Dawn
arms golden

9

for his
baskets soiled clothes

10

all around
Atthis
cloud

11

Truly, I wish I were dead.
She was weeping when she left me,

and said many things to me, and said this:
"How much we have suffered, Sappho.
Truly, I don't want to leave you."

And I answered her:
"Farewell. Go, and remember me.
You know how we care for you.

And if you should not, I want
to remind you
          of our moments of grace

the many garlands of violets,
roses and crocuses
          you put on my head,

the many necklaces
woven of flowers
          on my soft skin

all the myrrh
expensive
you anointed   royal

and on soft coverlets
tender
quenched your desire

nor ever any
shrine
from which we held back

nor grove   dance
          noise

12

sandals
of fine Lydian make, rainbow-dyed,
strapped to her feet

13

and for you I make an offering
of a white goat

14

Delicate Adonis is dying, Cytherea; what shall we do?
Beat your breasts, maidens, and rend your tunics.

15

either Cyprus or Paphos or Panormus
detains you

16

and I long and yearn

17

heart
completely
I can
may it be mine
to shine on me
your face
close whistling

18

you shrank
laurel when
everything sweeter
than that
and for the girls
traveler
scarcely ever heard
soul beloved
to be such now
to come gentle
you got there first, beautiful
and the clothes

19

Black dream
you come when sleep comes,
sweet god, truly dreadful agony

20

Look at him, just like a god,
that man sitting across from you,
whoever he is,
listening to your
close, sweet voice,
your irresistible laughter
And O yes,
it sets my heart racing—
one glance at you
and I can't get any words out,
my voice cracks,
a thin flame runs under my skin,
my eyes go blind,
my ears ring,
a cold sweat pours down my body,
I tremble all over,
turn paler than grass.
Look at me
just a shade from dead

But I must bear it, since a poor

21

Sappho, I love you
Cyprus   queen
and yet great
all upon whom the sun
everywhere fame
even in Acheron's
you

22

Stars around the full moon
hide their brilliant forms
when she bathes the world
in silver light.

23

Towards you, lovely ones, my thoughts
never change

24

From Cyprus
A herald came
Idaeus swift messenger:

"From the rest of Asia undying fame
Hector and his cohorts lead her dancing-eyed
from sacred Thebes and out of Plakos,
delicate Andromache, in ships over the salt
sea, with many golden bracelets and clothing
shining purple, necklaces, jewels of many colors,
countless silver cups and ivory."
He spoke, and Hector's old father rose nimbly,
and the word spread throughout the broad city
to his dear ones, and the Trojan women yoked mules
to their gliding chariots and went out in crowds
together with the slender-ankled girls,
Priam's daughters in a separate procession,
and the bachelors hitched up horses to their chariots,
young heroes in their might
charioteers
like gods
holy throng
to Ilion

and there rose
flute's melody sweet with the lyre
the rattle of castanets and shrill the maidens
sang the holy song and it reached bright heaven
eerie sound
and everywhere in the streets
mixing bowls and cups
myrrh and cassia and frankincense blended
and the older women with their alleluias
and all the men chanting the paeon
calling on Apollo his lyre his bright bow
praised Hector and Andromache, praised them as gods

25

robe
saffron
purple robe
cloaks
garlands
beautiful
purple

26

Eros has shaken my mind,
wind sweeping down the mountain on oaks

27

I will arrange my limbs
on soft cushions.

28

as long as you are willing

29

earth embroidered with flowers

30

I have a beautiful child, graceful
as golden flowers, my precious Kleis,
whom I would not trade for all of Lydia
or lovely Lesbos

31

Some say an army on horseback,
some say on foot, and some say ships
are the most beautiful things
on this black earth,
but I say
it is whatever you love.

It's easy to show this. Just look
at Helen, beautiful herself
beyond everything human,
and she left
her perfect husband and went
sailing off to Troy
without a thought for her child
or her dear parents, led astray

lightly

reminding me of Anactoria,
who is gone
and whose lovely walk
and bright
shimmering face
I would rather see
than all the chariots
and armed men in Lydia

but it cannot be

humans
pray to share

unexpectedly

32

I talked with you in a dream, Aphrodite.

33

hoping for love

for when I look at you face to face
not even Hermione can compare,
and it is no slight to liken you
to golden Helen.

mortal women; and know this
from all my cares

dewy banks
awake all night

34

night

maidens
all night long
might sing of your love
            and the violet-breasted bride's

35

Wreathe your lovely hair with garlands, Dika,
weave stems of anise with your tender hands.
The Graces love to see you crowned with flowers,
but they will turn away from your unwreathed head.

36

Sweet mother, I can no longer work the loom.
Slender Aphrodite has made me fall in love with a boy.

37

for you were once a child
come sing and dance
and favor us

for we are going to a wedding, and well
do you too but send away
the maidens as quickly as you can
and may the gods have

road to great Olympus
for humans

38

What farm girl has seduced you?
Draped in burlap,
she doesn't even know to pull her rags
down over her ankles.

39

For me neither honey nor the honey bee

40

Do I still put on virginity?

41

I do not know what to do; I am of two minds.

42

Raise high the roofbeam, carpenters,
Here comes the bride
Raise it up high,
Here comes the bride
Like Ares comes the groom,
Here comes the bride
Taller far than a tall man,
Here comes the bride

43

The best man's feet are seven yards long,
his sandals are made out of five oxhides,
ten cobblers wore themselves out on them.

44

To what shall I compare you, dear bridegroom?
I shall compare you to a slender sapling.

45

Virginity, virginity, where are you going,
deserting me?

I shall come to you no more, come no more.

46

a child, very soft, picking flowers

47

my mother once told me

that in her youth it was considered elegant
for a girl to put her hair up
in a purple headband—indeed it was—

but for the girl with hair more golden-red
than a flaming torch it was better
to do it up in wreaths of blooming flowers.

Recently an embroidered headband
from Sardis
Ionian cities

But, Kleis, I don't know where to get
An embroidered headband for you.
the Mytilenean, though

to get
embroidery

reminders of
exile of Cleanax's sons

dreadful loss

48

Hesperos, you bring all that the bright dawn scattered,
the lamb, the kid, the child to its mother.

fairest of stars

49

I loved you once, Atthis, long ago.
You seemed like a child to me, little and graceless.

50

“I want to say something, but shame
prevents me.”

“But if your desire were for the noble and good
and if your tongue were not brewing evil,
shame would not turn your eyes glassy
and you would speak out for what is right.”

51

He who is beautiful is beautiful only when seen,
But he who is good will be beautiful at once.

52

handkerchiefs
purple   scented
from Phocaea
expensive gifts

53

enough smoothness

the wind
curse
until the branch
while I live

54

from Sardis
often turning your mind here

we thought you were like a goddess
everyone looked at you
she loved the way you moved in the dance

now among the women of Lydia

as at sunset the rose-fingered moon
outshines all stars, spreading her light
over the salt sea, the flowering fields,

and the glimmering dew falls, roses
bloom amid delicate starflowers
chervil and sweet clover

she walks back and forth, remembering
her beloved Atthis,
the tender soul consumed with grief

to go there this
mind much
talks in the middle

It is not easy for us to equal
goddesses in beauty

Aphrodite
poured nectar from
a golden
Persuasion

the Geraesteum
dear ones

nothing

55

I do not expect any girl who looks upon
the sunlight
will ever have such skill

56

the beautiful and the good

        you   pain
    reproach
you swell
        you are grieved   for it

not so me
        she is disposed
                I understand
                disgrace
                other
        minds well
                blessed

57

Cypris and the Nereids
grant that my brother come back
unharmed to me
                    and that all be done
            as his heart desires

and grant, Immortal One, that he requite all
and be a delight to his friends
                    and   to his enemies
            and may no one be to us

and may he wish his sister to be honored
                    the painful hurt
            pouring it out
hearing   millet-seed

                    of the townsmen
in vain   again not
                    but you, Cypris,
disposing of the evil woman

58

You have forgotten me,
or you love someone else more.

59

Atthis,
you have come to hate the very thought of me,
and you run off to Andromeda.

60

hurt
work
face honored
winter storm

Abanthis, take your lyre and sing
of Gongyla, while desire once again
flutters around
the beautiful girl: her dress
excited you when you saw it,
and I am glad,
for the holy Cyprian herself
blamed me when I prayed

this word

I want

61

you came and you did it, and I wanted you
and you thoroughly deceived my mind
as it blazed with desire

62

But if you are my friend,
Go to a younger woman's bed;
For I will not endure an affair
In which I am older than the man.

63

sleeping on the chest of your tender companion

64

in my dripping pain

may aching winds carry off
my enemy

65

singeing us

66

bitten

with all your names

wins for your mouth
lovely gifts children
song-lover, lyre-shell
old age already all my skin
my hair turned white from black
knees do not bear
like fawns
but what could I do?
impossible to become
rose-armed Dawn
carrying to the ends of the earth
yet seized
immortal bedmate
thinks
might give
but I love delicacy, and love has won for me
the light of the sun, the sunlight's beauty

67

Spring's herald, the sweet-voiced nightingale

68

Why, Irana, does Pandion's daughter,
the swallow, waken me?

69

Like the sweet apple reddening on the topmost branch,
the topmost apple on the tip of the branch,
and the pickers forgot it,
well, no, they didn't forget, they just couldn't reach it.

Like the hyacinth in the hills the shepherds
trample, and on the ground the purple blooms

70

The moon rose full,
and when the women stood in place
around the altar

71

Eros once more limbslackener makes me shudder
sweetbitter   irresistible   creeping

the black sword of night in my eyes

73

The moon has set,
And the Pleiades.
Midnight.
The hour has gone by.
I sleep alone.

Notes on Ancient Sources

1 (Campbell 1) Dionysius of Halicarnassus, a first-century Greek literary critic and historian, quotes this poem as an example of "polished and exuberant" style in his work *On Literary Composition.*

2 (Campbell 21) This fragment survives on a second-century C.E. papyrus discovered at Oxyrhynchus in Egypt at the beginning of the 20th century. Over two-thirds of all surviving literary papyri have come from Oxyrhynchus (P. Oxy. 1231 fr. 10).

3 (Campbell 17) From a second-century C.E. papyrus from Oxyrhynchus (P. Oxy. 1231 fr. 1).

4 (Campbell 52) Herodian (second-century C.E.), one of the greatest original Greek grammarians, quotes this fragment in his work *On Anomalous Words* in reference to Sappho's spelling of the Greek word *oranos*, "sky."

5 (Campbell 55) Stobaeus includes this selection in a discussion of folly in his *Anthology*, a collection of excerpts (probably gathered in the early fifth-century C.E.) from poets and prose writers.

6 (Campbell 2) This poem survives as an inscription on a third-century B.C.E potsherd.

7 (Campbell 15) From a second-century C.E. papyrus found at Oxyrhynchus in Egypt (P. Oxy. 1231 fr. 1).

8 (Campbell 6) From a second-century C.E. Oxyrhynchus papyrus (P. Oxy. 2289 fr. 1).

9 (Campbell 7) From a second-century C.E. Oxyrhynchus papyrus (P. Oxy. 2289 fr. 2).

10 (Campbell 8) From a second-century C.E. Oxyrhynchus papyrus (P. Oxy. 2289 fr. 3).

11 (Campbell 94) This poem survives on a parchment from the sixth-century C.E.

12 (Campbell 39) A scholiast (an ancient commentator who wrote notes in and around the main text) preserved this fragment in the margins of a manuscript of Aristophanes' play *Peace*. Aristophanes was a fifth-century B.C.E. Greek comedic playwright.

13 (Campbell 40) Apollonius Dyscolus, a second-century C.E. grammarian, uses this line as an example of the Greek word *soi*, "to you," in his work *On Pronouns.*

14 (Campbell 140) Hephaestion, a second-century C.E. grammarian, quotes this in his *Handbook on Meter* to illustrate a catalectic line.

15 (Campbell 35) Strabo, a late first-century B.C.E. historian and geographer, incorporates this line of Sappho into his *Geography.*

16 (Campbell 36) This phrase is recorded in the *Etymologicum Genuinum*, a ninth–tenth-century C.E. work on the origins and meanings of words.

17 (Campbell 4) From a seventh-century C.E. parchment (P. Berol. 5006).

18 (Campbell 62) From a third-century C.E. Oxyrhynchus papyrus (P. Oxy. 1787 fr. 3).

19 (Campbell 63) From a third-century C.E. Oxyrhynchus papyrus (P. Oxy. 1787 fr. 3).

20 (Campbell 31) Longinus, a first-century C.E. critic who writes about the quality of thought and style (including the emotional element) that makes writing sublime, uses this poem in his work *On the Sublime* to illustrate excellence resulting from carefully chosen and combined details.

21 (Campbell 65) From a third-century C.E. Oxyrhynchus papyrus (P. Oxy. 1787 fr. 4).

22 (Campbell 34) Eustathius, a 12th-century C.E. bishop and scholar, quotes these lines of Sappho in a discussion about the moon in his commentary on Homer's *Iliad* (8.555).

23 (Campbell 41) Apollonius Dyscolus uses this line in his book *On Pronouns* to illustrate the Aeolic form of the word *ummin*, "to you."

24 (Campbell 44) From a third-century C.E. papyrus found at Oxyrynchus (P. Oxy. 1232 fr. 1).

25 (Campbell 92) From a sixth-century C.E. parchment (P. Berol. 9722).

26 (Campbell 47) Maximus of Tyre, a second-century C.E. author of essays with philosophical themes, quotes this in his *Orations.*

27 (Campbell 46) Herodian quotes this in *On Anomalous Words* in a discussion of Sappho's word for "cushion."

28 (Campbell 45) Apollonius Dyscolus uses this line in his book *On Pronouns* to illustrate the Aeolic form *ummes*, "you."

29 (Campbell 168c) This fragment is quoted in a work entitled *On Style*, a book of literary criticism. Although *On Style* is traditionally attributed to Demetrius of Phalerum (born c. 350 B.C.E.), the authorship is not certain.

30 (Campbell 132) Hephaestion includes this fragment in his book *Handbook on Meter* to explain aspects of trochaic meter.

31 (Campbell 16) From a second-century C.E. Oxyrhynchus papyrus (P. Oxy. 1231 fr. 1).

32 (Campbell 134) Hephaestion quotes this fragment in his *Handbook on Meter* to illustrate acatalectic meter.

33 (Campbell 23) From a second-century C.E. Oxyrhynchus papyrus (P. Oxy. 1231 fr. 14).

34 (Campbell 30) From a second-century C.E. Oxyrhynchus papyrus (P. Oxy. 1231 fr. 56).

35 (Campbell 81) Explaining why we should should wear garlands, Athenaeus (second–third-century C.E.) quotes these lines in *The Learned Banquet.*

36 (Campbell 102) Hephaestion quotes these lines in his *Handbook on Meter* as an example of an antispastic meter.

37 (Campbell 27) From a second-century C.E. Oxyrhynchus papyrus (P. Oxy. 1231 frr. 50–4).

38 (Campbell 57) Athenaeus quotes this in his *The Learned Banquet*, with the remark that Sappho is deriding her rival Andromeda.

39 (Campbell 146) Tryphon quotes this in his work *Figures of Speech* as an example of a proverb.

40 (Campbell 107) Apollonius Dyscolus quotes this fragment in his work *Conjunctions* to illustrate Sappho's spelling of an interrogative conjunction.

41 (Campbell 51) Chrysippus quotes this in his work *On Negatives.*

42 (Campbell 111) Hephaestion employs this fragment as an example of central refrain in his work *On Poems.*

43 (Campbell 110) In his *Handbook on Meter*, Hephaestion quotes these lines as a type of catalectic meter.

44 (Cambell 115) This is another example of a catalectic meter mentioned by Hephaestion in his *Handbook on Meter.*

45 (Campbell 114) This fragment is quoted by the author of *On Style* (see note on fragment 29) to demonstrate effective use of repetition.

46 (Campell 122) Athenaeus, in *The Learned Banquet*, includes this line of Sappho in a discussion of flower gathering.

47 (Campbell 98) The first lines (ending at "Ionian cities") come from a third-century B.C.E. papyrus (P. Haun. 301), the oldest extant papyrus of Sappho, now in Copenhagen. The remainder of the poem is from another papyrus fragment housed in Milan (P. Mediol. ed. Vogliano).

48 (Campbell 104) The beginning lines of this poem appear in *On Style*. The final fragment is quoted by Himerius, a fourth-century C.E. rhetorician, in his *Orations*.

49 (Campbell 49) The first line is quoted by Hephaestion in his *Handbook on Meter* as an example of the Sapphic fourteen-syllable meter. Plutarch, a second-century C.E. philosopher and biographer, quotes the second line in his *Dialogue on Love*. The two lines are written together as a unit by scholiasts in the margins of the Hephaestion text.

50 (Campbell 137) Aristotle (fourth-century B.C.E.) quotes these lines in a discussion on shame in his *Rhetoric*. He attributes (probably wrongly) the first two lines to the poet Alcaeus, a contemporary of Sappho.

51 (Campbell 50) Galen quotes these lines in his *Exhortation to Learning*.

52 (Campbell 101) Athenaeus quotes these lines in a reference to handkerchiefs in *The Learned Banquet*.

53 (Campbell 9) From a second-century C.E. Oxyrhynchus papyrus (P. Oxy. 2289 fr. 4).

54 (Campbell 96) From a sixth-century C.E. parchment (P. Berol. 9722 fol. 5).

55 (Campbell 56) Chrysippus (third-century B.C.E.), Stoic philosopher, quotes this in his work *Negatives*.

56 (Campbell 3) From a seventh-century C.E. parchment and a third-century C.E. Oxyrynchus papyrus (P. Berol. 5006 and P. Oxy. 424).

57 (Campbell 5) From a third-century C.E. Oxyrynchus papyrus (P. Oxy. 7 and 2289.6).

58 (Campbell 129) Apollonius Dyscolus quotes this in his work *On Pronouns* to illustrate a form of the Greek word for "me."

59 (Campbell 131) Hephaestion quotes these lines in his *Handbook on Meter* as examples of tetrameter verse.

60 (Campbell 22) From a second-century C.E. Oxyrynchus papyrus (P. Oxy. 1231 frr. 12, 15).

61 (Campbell 48) Julian the Apostate, Roman emperor 361–3 C.E., includes these lines in a letter to Iamblichus, a Neoplatonist philosopher.

62 (Campbell 121) Stobaeus, in his *Anthology*, quotes these lines in a discussion of age differences in love.

63 (Campbell 126) This fragment is quoted in the *Etymologicum Genuinum* in reference to an unusual word for "sleep."

64 (Campbell 37) Both of these fragments appear in the *Etymologicum Genuinum*. The first is in a discussion of the Greek word *stalagmos*, "dripping." The second fragment illustrates a dialect consonant change in the Greek word *epiplesso*, "carry off."

65 (Campbell 38) Apollonius Dyscolus quotes this fragment in his *On Pronouns* to illustrate the Aeolic form of the Greek word for "us."

66 (Campbell 58) From a third-century C.E. Oxyrhynchus papyrus (P. Oxy 1787 fr. 1).

67 (Campbell 136) A scholiast commenting on the play *Electra* (by the fifth-century B.C.E. Greek tragedian Sophocles) remarks on a similarity of expression concerning the nightingale by quoting this line of Sappho.

68 (Campbell 135) In his *Handbook on Meter*, Hephaestion uses this line to exemplify an ionic meter.

69 (Campbell 105) Syrianus, a fifth-century C.E. rhetorician and Neoplatonist philosopher, includes the first portion of this poem in a commentary he wrote on the book *On Kinds of Style*, authored by Hermogenes, a second-century C.E. critic. The final two lines are quoted by the author of *On Style* (see note 29).

70 (Campbell 154) This fragment is quoted by Hephaestion in his *Handbook on Meter* as an example of a particular type of trimeter line.

71 (Campbell 130) In his *Handbook on Meter* Hephaestion uses these lines to illustrate one variety of dactylic tetrameter.

72 (Campbell 151) From the *Etymologicum Genuinum* in reference to a rare word for "sleep." The translation follows a variant reading that suggests the word "sword."

73 (Campbell 168b) Hephaestion includes this fragment of Sappho in his *Handbook on Meter* to demonstrate a type of ionic tetrameter.